Narcissistic Abuse Recovery

The Survival Guide to Recognize Codependent Relationships, Disarming the Narcissists and Preventing Emotional Abuses

Markus Muller

derived from various sources. Please consult a licensed professional before attempting any techniques outlined in this book.

By reading this document, the reader agrees that under no circumstances is the author responsible for any losses, direct or indirect, which are incurred as a result of the use of information contained within this document, including, but not limited to, — errors, omissions, or inaccuracies.

Table of the contents:

Introduction

Narcissism, also known as Narcissistic Personality Disorder (NPD), is a mental illness characterized by a pattern of grandiosity. This individual is preoccupied and captivated with himself and continually wants to be adored. In addition to lacking sympathy and empathy, the narcissistic person is harsh, egocentric, and seeks domination and fulfillment. Dealing with and living with a narcissistic relationship can be extremely traumatic, owing to the emotional abuse that the narcissistic spouse has perpetrated. If you were married to a narcissist, you could find it tough to get out of that situation. If you manage to flee, you'll have a long and terrible rehabilitation ahead of you. You must persevere no matter how arduous the path to recovery is to get your life back on track.

What is Narcissism?

The term "narcissist" is frequently used in casual conversations to characterize someone who appears to be a little self-absorbed. However, to be diagnosed with narcissistic personality disorder in terms of clinical mental health, someone must fulfil a certain requirement.

Traits

People with narcissistic personality disorder are focused on their achievement and have an inflated sense of self-importance, which affects their decisionmaking and relations.

Because of their manipulative tendencies and lack of empathy, narcissists find it difficult to form or sustain relationships with others. They frequently have a sense of entitlement and lack compassion, but they want attention and adoration.

Here are some elements of narcissism:

- Having a feeling of grandeur or self-importance.

- Having delusions of becoming powerful, well-known, and/or significant.

- They're exaggerating their skills, capabilities, and achievements.

- I'm yearning for recognition and appreciation.

- Being obsessed with things like beauty, love, power, and/or success.

- Having an excessive feeling of one's own individuality.

- Believing that they owe anything to the rest of the world. Taking advantage of others to acquire what they want (no matter how it impacts others).

- Empathy for others is lacking.

What Is a Covert Narcissist?

In psychology, conduct is classified as either overt or covert. Overt actions, such as those of the classic narcissist outlined above, are ones that others can easily witness. Covert behaviors, on the other hand, are more subtle and less visible to others.

A covert narcissist desires adulation and power while lacking empathy for others but behaves differently from an overt narcissist.

When contemplating narcissist conduct, it's challenging to comprehend how someone may be a narcissist while still being constrained in their approach and conduct. For example, the approach of a covert narcissist might be overtly self-effacing or aloof, but the end aims are the same.

For example, this may be contrasted to listening to your favorite music at full volume or listening to the same music at a low level. The music hasn't changed;

It's simply the level at which you're listening that has.

Overt vs Covert

The sole difference between covert and overt narcissists is that covert narcissists are more introverted. The overt narcissist is easy to spot because they are loud, arrogant, and oblivious to the needs of others, and they are always eager for accolades. 1

Others may quickly notice their actions, and they appear to be "large" in a room. Thus, when we think of an overt narcissist, we could think of someone who engages in more outgoing social interactions.

Craig Malkin, PhD, a researcher and author, believes that the term "covert" might be deceptive. In his study, he claims that the word covert is frequently used to imply that a covert narcissist is sly or that their desire for power isn't as strong as an overt (more extroverted) narcissist's. But he claims that overt and covert narcissists have the same characteristics.

Narcissists, both hidden and overt, go around with a feeling of selfimportance and fantasize about achievement and grandeur.

Both persons must fulfill the same clinical criteria to be diagnosed with a narcissistic personality disorder, whether extroverted or introverted. Both have problems controlling their self-esteem.

Many individuals have been victims of covert narcissism's manipulative activities without even recognizing it until they are in emotional distress. Therefore, it's probably more realistic to say that the extroverted (overt) narcissist is simpler to spot than the introverted (covert) narcissist.

It's very uncommon for people to find themselves in long-term relationships with hidden narcissists, only to be disappointed by a lack of cooperation or reciprocity.

Somatic vs Cerebral

The second sub-type defines the narcissist's most essential values in himself and others. No narcissist wants their mate to outshine them. Their companion is seen as a dazzling thing that they may flaunt to boost their social prestige. Somatic narcissists, who are concerned with their bodies and looks, and cerebral narcissists, who pretend to be know-it-alls, are both members of this sub-type. They consider themselves the most intelligent persons in the room and like impressing others with their achievements. Classic narcissists, susceptible narcissists, communal narcissists, and malignant narcissists can all be somatic or intellectual.

Inverted vs Sadistic

There are a few different sorts of narcissists in the last and last sub-type. The inverted narcissist is the first specific sub-type, which exclusively applies to fragile, covert narcissists. This subgroup of narcissists is codependent and prefers to associate with other narcissists in order to feel unique. In addition, they have a victim mentality and have trouble with child abandonment.

The sadistic narcissist, a sub-type of a malignant narcissist, is the second specific sub-type. This group is similar to sociopaths and psychopaths in that they revel in the suffering of others. In addition, they like humiliating and injuring others, and they may have strange sexual preferences.

Signs to Look For

Although specific clinical criteria must be satisfied in order for someone to be diagnosed with narcissistic personality disorder, if you feel you're dealing with a covert narcissist, there are certain basic qualities and patterns to watch for in everyday encounters.

Being aware of these characteristics might assist individuals who engage with the covert narcissist recognize and navigate potentially harmful situations.

Passive Self-Importance

The overt, extroverted narcissist is more visible in their enhanced sense of self and arrogance while engaging with others, whereas the covert narcissist is less visible.

Although the covert narcissist desires status and adoration, it might appear differently to people around them. They may provide backhanded compliments or purposely downplay their successes or capabilities to get comfortable about their abilities.

The fact is that narcissists, both overt and covert, have a weak sense of self.

The overt narcissist will demand adoration and attention, but the covert narcissist will employ subtler methods to achieve the same ends. The covert narcissist will be far more likely to seek reinforcement about their abilities, skills, and successes regularly, searching for others to satisfy their desire for self-importance.

Blaming and Shaming

The narcissist's favorite method for maintaining their sense of superiority regarding others is to shame people. However, the overt (extroverted) narcissist's technique to acquiring power may be more visible, such as putting you down, being impolite, criticizing you, and being sarcastic.

The introverted, covert narcissist may take a kinder approach to explain why something is your fault and not theirs. They may even act as if they are victims of your actions or participate in emotional abuse to obtain reassurance and admiration from you. The narcissist's purpose is to make the other person feel tiny at the end of these conversations.

Creating Confusion

Although not necessarily cunning, some covert narcissists enjoy perplexing the person with whom they are communicating. Instead of accusing or humiliating, they may cause individuals to reconsider their assumptions and second-guess themselves.

Another approach for the covert narcissist to gain influence over another person is to utilize strategies like this to elevate themselves and retain power in the relationship. If they can persuade you to rethink your beliefs, they will have additional opportunities to control and exploit you.

Procrastination and Disregard

Because their need for self-importance is so strong, covert narcissists will go to any length to keep the spotlight on themselves. Whereas an extroverted narcissist would brazenly push you aside or manipulate you to achieve their objective, the covert narcissist is a master at ignoring you completely.

It's no surprise that narcissists, in general, like to engage with individuals who are kind and empathetic. Unfortunately, those chances for manipulation are also recognized by the covert narcissist.

They have no qualms about telling you that you are insignificant.

Rather than telling you directly that you're unimportant, they may cancel a date, react to messages or emails late, often show up late for activities with you, or never make definite plans with you at all. As a result, there is no consideration for your time or interests, making you feel insignificant, inconsequential, and irrelevant.

Emotionally Neglectful

Narcissists are terrible at forming and maintaining emotional ties with other people. If their energy is always focused on themselves, how could they sustain ties with others? A concealed narcissist is no exception. They are not emotionally available or receptive while appearing gentler and less irritating than their extroverted counterpart.

A hidden narcissist is unlikely to shower you with flattery. It's simple to see why a covert narcissist might find complimenting you difficult, given their constant concentration on being elevated to preserve their feeling of self importance. The narcissist typically has little regard for your qualities or abilities— in fact, the narcissist frequently has none at all.

In a relationship with covert narcissists, you'll likely find yourself performing most of the hard emotional work, just as you would with overt narcissists. However, although the covert is more likely to look emotionally accessible, it is frequently a performance done to exploit or make the person feel small through dismissiveness, belittling, or humiliating.

The hidden narcissist will not be emotionally receptive to their spouse in a healthy way since one of the fundamental qualities of narcissistic personality disorder is a lack of empathy.

Giving With a Goal

Narcissists, on the whole, are not givers. They have a hard time putting their focus into something that does not benefit them in some manner. A covert narcissist may appear to be generous, but their giving conduct is solely to receive something in return.

Putting a tip in the jar at your neighborhood coffee shop is a simple, daily example. When a covert narcissist knows the barista is watching, they are far more likely to place their tip in the jar in order to establish some type of contact that allows them to be complimented for giving.

Giving is always more about them for a covert narcissist than it is about people to whom they are giving.

Other Types Of Narcissism

What are the different varieties of narcissism?

While narcissistic personality disorder (NPD) can be identified, there is no clinical diagnostic for any of the subtypes of narcissism. Some varieties of narcissism have been recognized and promoted informally by various mental health practitioners, while others have been discovered and verified through peer-reviewed research. As a result, there isn't a set number of narcissistic subtypes.

Craig Malkin, PhD, a clinical psychologist and Harvard lecturer, views narcissism as a characteristic, or persistent human propensity, that occurs on a scale.

Psychologist Perpetua Neo, DClinPsy, says mental health doctors "can typically discern patterns" even if the subtypes can't be clinically identified.

Experts have identified eight forms of narcissism:

1. Healthy Narcissism

Yes, there is such a thing as healthy narcissism. A narcissistic personality disorder is not the same as having narcissistic tendencies. To be clinically diagnosed with NPD, a person must display at least 55 percent of the most prevalent indicators of narcissism, according to the Diagnostic and Statistical Manual

(DSM-5). Unfortunately, many people exhibit narcissistic characteristics without matching the diagnostic criteria for the disease. Healthy narcissism is a distinct type that is genuinely beneficial.

At mbg, cognitive therapist Alyssa Mancao, LCSW, says, "Each individual has a little of healthy narcissism within them."

A person with healthy narcissism is proud of their achievements and wants to share them with others because it makes them feel good. Healthy narcissism also includes feeling entitled to specific settings and believing that you deserve excellent things. These sensations, on the other hand, are typically accurate."

2. Grandiose Narcissism

Grandiose narcissism is quite similar to the general definition of a narcissist. Grandiosity is a psychological term that refers to a false sense of superiority. Overestimating one's talents, expressing one's power over others, and having a generally exaggerated sense of self-esteem are all examples of grandiose narcissism.

In contrast to susceptible narcissism, this kind of narcissism has been studied and verified by peer-reviewed research (also known as covert narcissism).

"Grandiose narcissism occurs when a person's narcissistic characteristics— entitlement, braggadocio, and self-obsession— are publicly shown, frequently at the expense of others," according to the definition. Neo declares. Although grandiose narcissists might be seductive, they frequently lack empathy. They don't relate to individuals in talks, Neo explains, but rather one-up them. This might be due to a need for attention, a desire to see others upset and confused, or both.

It's critical to establish boundaries while dealing with a grandiose narcissist, or any narcissist for that matter. Neo advises, "Know that you may be gracious and aggressive at the same moment." "They'll test your limits, reducing them to the point when a reduced degree of care becomes the new normal. So prepare to stand firm in your boundaries—or, better still, walk away."

3. *Vulnerable Narcissism, Also Known As Covert Narcissism*

Vulnerable narcissism is another term for covert narcissism. These people, in contrast to grandiose narcissists, are quiet and self-effacing. The "covert subtype is constrained, clearly upset, hypersensitive to others' opinions while constantly jealous," according to the American Journal of Psychiatry (AJP). They desire attention from others and get defensive when confronted with criticism.

Covert narcissists, according to Malkin, are frequently sad and feel their misery is worse than anybody else's. "Yes, they've been harmed before," Neo explains, "but it's not your responsibility to rescue or save them." That, too, is a matter of limits."

4. *Malignant narcissism*

Malignant narcissists are manipulative and malevolent, as the word indicates. They exhibit sadism and aggressiveness and are the most severe kind of narcissistic personality disorder, according to AJP.

"Seeing others writhe in pain and anguish gives them pleasure," says licensed psychologist Daniel Fox, PhD. If you know a malignant narcissist, Neo advises absolutely ignoring them and breaking all relations with them. "They've spent their lives practicing the technique of becoming greater narcissists," she argues, so any effort to outwit them would be futile and tiresome.

5. *Sexual Narcissism*

According to couples' therapist Brandon Santan, PhD, sexual narcissists "have an extremely enthusiastic, narcissistic appreciation of their own sexual skill." "Their fixation with sexual performance and the need for others' sexual praise can devour them."

Serial cheaters, those who use sex to control others, and those who act aggressively during sex are all characteristics of sexual narcissists. To protect yourself against this sort of narcissist, the best thing you can do is leave the relationship and get treatment to help you cope with the breakup.

Sexual narcissism is one of three types of narcissism that comprise sexual narcissism, somatic narcissism, and intellectual narcissism. Although none have been scientifically confirmed, the system has grown in favor as some mental health professionals better utilize it to identify distinct varieties of narcissism.

6. *Somatic Narcissism*

The self-worth of somatic narcissists is derived from their bodies. "This may show as someone feeling more handsome, stronger, or fitter than others," explains psychotherapist Christine Scott-Hudson, LMFT.

Somatic narcissists are generally obsessed with their weight and physical attractiveness, and they criticize others for it. In addition, they frequently disregard the needs of others in favor of their own. "Avoid expressing emotional responses to their actions because narcissists live off drama," Scott-Hudson advises if you're dealing with one.

7. *Cerebral Narcissist*

The self-importance of cerebral or intellectual narcissists is derived from their minds, whereas the self-importance of somatic narcissists is derived from their bodies. Thus, cerebral narcissists get their fix by convincing themselves that they are brighter, cleverer, and more intelligent than others.

Narcissists who feel they are smarter than others are known as cerebral narcissists. They will strive to make others appear stupid to feed their ego. When dealing with a cerebral narcissist, keep your distance from their remarks. "You'll never win an argument or persuade them to realize you're right," Fox adds, "so learn to let it go."

8. *Spiritual Narcissist*

According to Neo, spiritual narcissists frequently exploit their spirituality to rationalize bad acts and employ spiritual language to frighten others. "See, the narcissist has to create an idealized picture of himself to escape his shattered, insecure nature," she explains, adding that spiritual narcissists utilize ostensibly sensitive and spiritual activities to raise themselves above others.

Young individuals and those who have gone through considerable upheavals, such as a move or a divorce, are more susceptible to spiritual narcissists' "captivating, dynamic influence," according to Neo. Therefore, separate yourself from anyone who exploits their faith to exploit or denigrate you.

There are many distinct varieties of narcissism, some of which are more concerning than others, and narcissism occurs on a scale. For example, suppose you're dealing with someone you believe has a narcissistic personality disorder. In that case, the best thing you can do to protect yourself is set to clear boundaries and, preferably, end the relationship.

What's Codependency?

The word 'codependency' sounds like it stands for something positive— something mutually beneficial. If you had thought it was something good when you first heard the word, you are not alone.

Of course, codependency refers to something 'mutual,' but the 'beneficial' part is completely off.

There is nothing beneficial in a codependent relationship, neither is there anything beneficial for a codependent person. Indeed, a codependent person is someone whose relationship with himself or herself is in a state of deepseated self-doubt, whereby they no longer trust themselves. When a codependent relationship ends, one of the partners is likely to indulge in selfabuse, self-blame, self-shaming, and an inability to handle even the slightest form of criticism. This is usually a precursor to self-sabotaging or even suicidal behaviors.

In its basic form, codependency is excessive psychological or emotional reliance on another person who needs support because of an addiction or ill health. A codependent person allows another person's behavior to influence them significantly to the point of taking full responsibility for controlling the other person's behavior. The codependent person enables the dependent person in the relationship. That is to say, the codependent partner behaves in ways that encourage the other partner to continue in their irresponsibility, immaturity, addiction, and illness.

Codependency goes beyond mere clinginess.

A codependent person typically lives their life for their partner—their world revolves around the partner's world. They go to extreme lengths to please their partner. A codependent relationship is one in which one partner believes that their sense of purpose depends on the support given to the other person, and the other person believes that they need to be needed. The codependent partner usually engages in self-sacrificing behavior for the sake of their partner, who, incidentally, expects nothing less. The neediness by one partner and the need to feel needed by the other partner is known as the cycle of codependency.

Codependency is not restricted to romantic partners alone. It can happen between friends, family, and even colleagues at work too. In many cases, the relationship can degenerate into a physically and emotionally abusive one. Other people outside the relationship can often see that something is off, but the codependent partner usually doesn't realize it.

Codependency Is Not...

Codependency is not caregiving.

Many people can confuse the two because the word has been so overused in our lexicon that nearly all examples of kindness and caregiving are looked at as codependent when there is a huge difference. When someone is giving of their heart and, for example, taking care of a sick parent or child.

There is a big difference because they give of themselves to that person because they love them and want to see them get better.

These are specific situations.

This is not a pattern of relationships and dysfunction that they are getting into and seeking out even if they don't know they are seeking it out on a consistent basis. You can look at it almost as if one is chronic and one is acute.

Even if the acute situation turns into long-term caring. It is not because the caregiver is codependent. They are doing it out of love for a child, a parent, or whoever. It is important to not mistake kindness and love for codependency.

They are two different things. Some people are thrust into situations where they have to give of themselves, such as the examples mentioned above, they are not seeking them out, but they approach them with love and compassion, kindness, and a genuine giving of themselves to get that person back the way they were.

Look at it this way; codependency is something that a codependent person will seek out because that is all they know.

It is a compulsion to become involved with somebody in that type of relationship where you're going to give everything you have in order to please that person or take care of that person or control that person.

It is not coming from a place of love. It is coming from a place of need because, in a way, the codependent person satisfies their own need for acceptance and validation by being involved with this person.

On the other hand, the caregiving person is doing it out of genuine love, concern, and kindness. They are doing it because they feel compelled to help a loved one; it is not a compulsion.

It is really important to differentiate the two and understand the difference. It signifies a healthy response to a loved one in need and not to satisfy their own needs or compulsions.

It is to help and caregivers to the one that they love.

The codependence arises from shame. They will deny their own needs and feelings. They have a perfectionist attitude towards helping this person that they are involved with. Their low self-esteem keeps them around, and they have this insatiable need to please people and feel guilty if they do not act perfect. This is codependency.

The boundaries are just completely out of whack.

The healthy individual, on the other hand, is looking to care for the person.

They are doing it out of love. They are doing it out of genuine caring and concern, and kindness.

Codependency is fake proximity of what true love is. It's an obsessive, allconsuming need to please, win approval, and validation from others.

Just because you have the feelings of wanting to help others and to be there for your loved ones, that does not make you codependent.

To summarize, codependency is not caring and giving everything; we have to people that we love to see them happy or get them through a difficult time. Also, it is not when you are briefly hurt because someone betrayed you or that you want to see somebody improve and get better because they act in a destructive manner.

These are normal reactions.

This is just part of being human.

How People Become Codependent

Codependency is a learned behavior and can be passed down from generation to generation. It is imperative to understand what kinds of situations can cause a person to develop codependency to prevent this cycle from hurting more people. Many people learn to become codependent in order to survive their dysfunctional families. It can be used as a defense mechanism, a way to bring more order to the house, or a way to gain some control over what goes on in their lives. Along with dysfunctional families, abusive relationships can also cause a person to become codependent as well as being the partner of an addict, which was originally believed to be the only cause.

There are several types of relationships that can cause a person to develop codependent behavior.

- Romantic relationship with an addict
- Romantic relationship with an abusive person

- Growing up with a resentful parent

- Growing up with a narcissist

- Growing up with an addict

Romantic Relationship With An Addict

Having someone they love to fall into the deep hole of addiction can be really harmful to people. When they find out about their partner's addiction, feelings of jealousy and despair may arise in the partner of an addict, which then leads to developing codependency in the relationship. Everyone wants to help their loved ones when they are in trouble. However, codependent partners of addicts might not realize that their codependency is enabling the addict's behavior. They might realize that their partner comes home later, tries not to speak about their day too much, spends more of the family money than before, or otherwise partakes in other suspicious behavior.

Thinking that their partner must be cheating on them, they get jealous and angry. While they were thinking that their partner was having an affair, they realized it was something worse, addiction.

Finding out about the addiction makes the partner concerned about the addict's physical and mental health, so they naturally want to help the person they love. The partner of the addict starts to develop codependency after they offer a helping hand to the addict and start doing everything the addict needs so that they don't die, go to jail, or embarrass their family to other people. They want to be a 'good partner' in their addict's eyes so that one day when the addict gets sober, they will get have the partner to thank for taking care of them.

Seeing that all of the attention and love of the addict is going towards their addiction, the codependent partner feels resentment and jealousy, not towards the addict but towards the addiction of their choosing. The codependent starts to do things to be noticed and praised by the addict, like cleaning up after them, lying to the neighbors about the addict's behavior, and working extra hard to provide money for the house. Addicts can do crazy things to find the money for their addiction, and their codependent does not want them to get hurt, so sometimes the money the codependent giver makes may end up going towards the addict's addiction.

As much as this upsets the codependent, the fact that the addict needs them satisfies the codependent. However, they might not realize that all of the harm and consequences they are protecting the addict from are keeping the addict from seeing where addiction can take them. The addict doesn't go homeless because the codependent pays the rent, the addict doesn't go hungry because the codependent provides and cooks the food, the addict doesn't get harmed because the codependent giver is there to take care of them, and the addict doesn't have to live in filth because the codependent cleans up after them. Indeed, no sensible person would starve someone they love because they are an addict. But how could the addict know the adverse effects of their addiction if they never have to face them?

Nobody wants to believe that their partner wants to hurt them. It is like when a person gets cheated on; they might blame the person their partner cheated on them with for breaking up their happy relationship. They don't blame their partner because that would mean coming to terms with the fact that their partner wanted to share intimacy with someone other than them. Codependent partners of addicts feel just like a partner who has been cheated on. They resent the substance (drugs, alcohol, gambling, etc.) for taking their partner's love and affection from them and subconsciously try to get their partner to depend on them, the codependent giver, as much as the addiction.

This makes the codependent feel like their relationship has not totally failed or like they are still a part of their partner's life.

Example: While you wait for your dinner to finish cooking, you see your partner passed out in the living room with an empty bottle of wine next to them. You start thinking, when did your life become so hectic yet so lonely? You used to have friends to go out with, a favorite TV show to watch after work, and a career plan. Then your partner got fired from their job, couldn't find another one, and they started drinking.

It started out with a glass of wine after a long day of job hunting and turned into a couple of bottles of wine after half a day of job hunting. To help them through this challenging time, you decided not to be so harsh on them and support them until they could find another job. You thought the drinks were helping them not feel so horrible about their situation and assumed that it would stop as soon as they got a new job. You get a second job and pick up a couple of extra shifts at your full-time job to cover the finances until then.

Your partner tells you how much they appreciate you for being their rock and promises to make it all up to you once they get a new job.

Now here you are, a year later, and you are getting up at 5 am every day, cooking and leaving breakfast on the table, so your partner eats something after they wake up, working at a storage facility until 12 pm, and then heading to your second job as a sales assistant at the mall until 8. Today, you even stopped by the liquor store to pick up a couple of bottles of wine because you noticed there was only 1 left, and you didn't want your partner to drive while drunk to get some more. You come home after a long commute and start on the pile of laundry, clean the house, and cook dinner. Your partner is in the living room, passed out from drinking. They have not mentioned anything about applying for a new job in the last 6 months, and you stopped asking a long time ago because every time you asked, they'd break down crying about how hard it is, which made you feel terrible.

You didn't want your partner to suffer through their addiction, so you were ready to help them get through it. They said it themselves that they wouldn't be okay if it weren't for you. Sure, they only said it when you did something for them, and they didn't look that okay but hearing it still made you feel happy and loved. Maybe if you showed more love to your partner, they wouldn't have a hole to fill with drinking. You couldn't just give up on them; they needed you! Before you got up to get your food, your last thought was that maybe one day your partner will decide to get sober, and everything will go back to how it was, or maybe one day you will finally have enough of this and leave.

Codependents realize that they have to make "room" for the partner's addiction if they want their partner to pay attention to them. This makes the codependent feel like they are not essential or worthy of love unless they accommodate their partner's needs. To feel important in their partner's life, the codependent fulfills the addict's needs, and that causes the addict to feel more comfortable living with their addiction. In a way, codependency becomes an addiction for the codependent giver. Codependent behavior can be very damaging to a person suffering from addiction because it doesn't ask them to change or give them a sign that habit is bad.

Romantic Relationship With An Abusive Person

In many cases, people become codependent while they are growing up, but it is also common for people to develop codependency later in their lives. Abusive relationships can break a person down to a point they no longer recognize themselves. A confident, strong-minded person might see the red flags and run away when they see the first sign of abuse, but if a person has even just one symptom of codependency, such as low self-esteem, they might be more exposed to becoming codependent during an abusive relationship and never leave.

The word 'abuse' in relationships used to have a really restrictive meaning. For a relationship to be considered abusive, the man of the house had to be physically abusing the woman. Physically abusing a child was considered discipline, and if someone heard about a woman beating up a man, they laughed and shrugged it off. Since these times, we have evolved to understand how much more critical domestic abuse is, how much more inclusive it should be, and how big of a role abuse plays in a person's life.

Signs Of Narcissistic Abuse In A Broad Way

- Five Signs of Narcissism:
- Common Characteristics of Narcissistic Personalities
- Monopoly on Conversation
- Flaunting Rules or Social Conventions
- Unreasonable Expectations
- Fixation with Appearance
- Disregard for Other People
- Praise, Praise and More Praise
- It's Everyone Else's Fault
- They Fear Abandonment
- The Narcissist Lives in The Fantasy
- There Are Always Strings Attached

Despite its origins in ancient Greek mythology, the term "narcissist" now refers to persons who display specific characteristics linked with narcissistic personality disorder (NPD). The scientific community recognizes NPD as a psychiatric disorder, while there are many differing perspectives on contributing factors and treatments. Nevertheless, there are several traditional indicators of narcissism, some of which have severe negative consequences for friends, family members, and employees.

Movies like "Mommy Dearest," "American Psycho," "The Talented Mr. Ripley," and "The Wolf of Wall Street" have shown how narcissists operate in society. True, narcissists make for an intriguing night at the theater. However, detecting a narcissist in a movie is likely to be different from detecting one in real life. In the real world, the signs of narcissism aren't usually as obvious, at least not at first.

Psychologists have a variety of hypotheses regarding how and why certain people acquire narcissism. The underlying assumption of these ideas is that the narcissist suffers a major psychological wound early in life. This wound was frequently caused by trauma, like abuse or neglect. As a result, the narcissist created a fake identity. The narcissist's urge to defend this self at all costs causes many of the classic indications of narcissism.

While there are many indications for Narcissistic Personality Disorder:

The ten listed below are among the most frequent.

1. Monopoly on Conversation

In order to convey their opinions or talk about themselves, many narcissists talk over or interrupt other individuals during talks. This conduct might feel compulsion-like, lulling people into complete quiet for minutes at a time. Unfortunately, they tend to ignore or respond superficially to others' opinions before returning the conversation to their story.

Part of the narcissist's obsessive desire for admiration and the narcissist's sense of entitlement contribute to this tendency. It also has to do with the fact that narcissists often lack empathy. The fact that others want to be seen and heard is unimportant to the narcissist. A narcissist has the right to be the focus of attention at all times.

2. Flaunting Rules or Social Conventions

A drive to break conventions or traditions, often with spectacular results, is one of the more disruptive indications of narcissism. A narcissistic personality tends to demand special treatment in various situations and feels mistreated when not getting around the system. According to Psychology Today, this attitude may present itself in various ways, including breaking traffic regulations, stealing supplies at work, and cutting others in the line. In other words, the rules are in place for the benefit of others, not the narcissist. The narcissist is one of a kind. Because of their exceptional position, they are able to go around the regulations.

3. Fixation on Appearance

People with NPD, like the fabled Narcissus, acquire a great obsession with outer looks. Some people spend hours in front of the mirror every day, feeling obliged to continuously correct or change their looks. Narcissists are also more likely to make comments about other people's appearances or to make direct insults about their clothing, body type, or facial traits. People with narcissism are concerned with making huge impressions on others in addition to their physical attractiveness. This may cause people to exaggerate or manufacture stories in order to boost their perceived worth.

It is also possible that narcissists demand their family to be attractive. They can't be as attractive as the narcissist – think of the wicked queen in Snow White – but they must make the narcissist appear attractive by being attractive themselves. Those who fall short of the narcissistic parent's expectations are mistreated and bullied. Because they feel that a child is an extension of the parent, the narcissistic parent feels that these sentiments are legitimate. Narcissists' children exist to make their parents appear decent. They're useless outside of this. They don't have their own requirements or desires.

However, physical appearances are only one aspect of appearances. It is also crucial for a narcissist's life to seem immaculate. The narcissist's main ambition is to keep up with the Joneses. It's even better if the narcissist can outdo the Joneses.

4. Emphasis on Envy

Another basic characteristic of narcissism is a jealous mentality. While many individuals experience envy at times throughout their lives, narcissists might become entirely absorbed by these sentiments. They may continuously criticize other people's possessions or good fortune, or they may believe that other people are envious of them. Some narcissists utilize this impulse to seek out and mingle with affluent or famous individuals intentionally. Envy motivates narcissists to steal or minimize the labor of their coworkers in the workplace. It's possible that the narcissist didn't put much effort into a project. Nonetheless, the narcissist expects to see their name at the top of a project.

Narcissists may also believe that someone performing a better job than them owes them a break at work. The narcissist is envious of others' abilities, which they have gained through years of hard effort. If the narcissist is unable to learn such talents, they will gladly employ the talented individual. If the narcissist is unable to exploit someone to achieve their goals, the narcissist may attempt to drive that individual out of a job. This reduces the narcissist's competitiveness, at least temporarily.

5. Disregard for Other People

Manipulative behaviors are common among narcissists, who use their relations with others to achieve their own aims. People with the illness frequently form significant emotional bonds with friends or family members and then utilize those bonds to their advantage. This manipulation style may take many forms, including dramatic mood swings, heated disagreements, and a tendency to blame others.

If the narcissist senses a slight, this attitude might lead to the narcissist being enraged at others. If a member of the narcissist's family becomes ill, for example, the narcissist may be negligent at best and cruel at worst. Because the narcissist lacks empathy, imagining the suffering of others is difficult for him or her.

6. Praise, Praise and More Praise

The group's movie star is the narcissist. They expect to be adored everywhere they go. Narcissists also need frequent praise from others, even if it is undeserved. Narcissists guarantee that they obtain their narcissistic supply by situating and monopolizing the discourse. So be it if others feel cheated in the process. The narcissist obtains what they want regardless of the cost to others. This includes compliments.

Furthermore, as Healthline.com points out, if praises do not flow effortlessly, the narcissist will put himself in the way of them. The narcissist searches for compliments about their beauty, food, work, or life, sometimes referred to as fishing. Despite their outward confidence, they are consumed with self-doubt. They begin to feel slighted if praise is not given at regular intervals. This encourages them to seek out more praise.

Narcissists need someone who continuously elevates them. Their superficial appeal makes them a popular favorite early on, so praise comes more freely to them. On the other hand, the adoring phase never lasts long since the narcissist's demand for praise is insatiable. Unfortunately, if the narcissist does not receive the level of adulation that they desire, the narcissist will become enraged. This wrath is frequently the initial stage in the cycle of abuse for narcissists who turn physically violent.

If they can, narcissists will use charm to get admiration and acclaim. If they are unable to obtain what they believe they are entitled to, they resort to other, often extremely damaging and even dangerous, strategies. If the narcissist gets criticism, on the other hand, the situation can quickly become heated. Again, the narcissist could show signs of wrath that border on wrath.

Unfortunately, the person who was the target of the fury may not have even criticized the narcissist. Instead, the narcissist mistook the person's statement or action for an insult and retaliated. The narcissist's poor self-esteem causes all of this. Given the level of arrogance displayed by many narcissists, it's difficult for their victims to accept that the narcissists' low self-esteem is crippling. Yes, it does.

Many narcissists go to considerable efforts to boost their own ego and gain the attention they need. One of the most evident indications of narcissism is this. According to Psychology Today, some narcissists need praise and adulation so much that they choose high-profile positions in business or politics to satisfy this urge.

A broken and wounded inner child is the source of this obsessive want for attention. In trying to be accepted and feel comfortable in a hazardous situation, the youngster created a false self as a result of this wound. To the narcissist, an attack on their fake self seems like annihilation. Receiving comments and praise from others is how the narcissist puts these feelings of inadequacy at bay.

7. It's Everyone Else's Fault

According to Very Well Mind, shaming and blaming are two crucial techniques in the narcissist's manipulation kit.

The narcissist exercises power over their victims through these poisonous twins. In the view of the narcissist, making someone feel shame permits the narcissist to have a higher status in a relationship. For the victim, it's always a one-up position. If the victim disrupts the power balance in any way, the narcissist will go to great lengths to re-establish the power disparity in favor of the narcissist.

The narcissist gains power by being impolite, putting others down, hiding behind nasty jokes, criticizing, and undermining. For example, a person uncomfortable about their weight may become the brunt of the narcissist's fat jokes, or the narcissist may choose to be frank rather than make a joke.

The narcissist, on the other hand, typically disguises the comments as wellintentioned. For example, after shaming someone over their weight during a public meal, a narcissist can declare, "I'm only worried for your health."

When the victim objects, the narcissist shames them into silence by reminding them that the statement was made for their own benefit. To make a point, the narcissist can say the victim is too sensitive. This prevents the victim from defending themselves against the narcissist's abuse, exposing the victim to even more abuse. What's more alarming about some of these incidents is that this type of public humiliation creates the chance that others within earshot would follow suit. When this occurs, the victim is subjected to more than simply the narcissist's humiliating methods. They are subjected to the entire group's humiliation strategy.

There is also a propensity among more subtle narcissists to blame everyone else for the narcissist's conduct and flaws. The child who receives a "B" on their report card is held responsible for the parent's poor performance. The victim of physical violence is held responsible for the narcissist's behavior. The child's responsibility is if the narcissist has a neglected spouse since the child diverts the husband's attention away from the narcissist.

It is never the narcissist's fault in these situations. Everything that others do wrong reflects adversely on the narcissist, whether the insult is genuine or imagined. By blaming others, the narcissist absolves themselves of all responsibility for their life and acts. A narcissist is unlikely to recognize their participation in a terrible circumstance. People who refuse to follow the narcissist's internal, well-choreographed script intend to injure the narcissist. This is the narcissist's viewpoint.

However, most of the time, individuals around the narcissist are unaware of this mental script until the narcissist explodes when someone goes off-script. Such an attitude sets the narcissist up to continuously have someone to blame and abuse. It also places the narcissist in the driver's seat. People who are close to a narcissist must continually tread carefully. They never know when the narcissist may concoct a new crime to accuse them of, which keeps the narcissist's victims on their toes.

8. They Fear Abandonment

The majority of what a narcissist does is to ensure that they are never abandoned. The narcissist's biggest fear is being abandoned. However, as strange as it may sound, desertion frequently occurs at the hands of the narcissist, who may abruptly end relationships with individuals. It's often a matter of leaving before they can be abandoned in the mind of a narcissist.

Although the narcissist is the one who initiates the breakup, it seldom lasts. Victims of this split must recognize that various reasons contribute to the makeup cycle.

To begin with, the narcissist requires their narcissistic supply to feel good. Therefore, it only makes sense to the narcissist to return to someone they have already rejected. The narcissist has already educated that individual to give them the praise the narcissist craves.

Second, the process of leaving and repeatedly returning wears the victim down. The victim's self-esteem takes a serious knock after a while. The victim becomes reliant on the narcissist while the pattern of leaving and returning continues. This assures that the narcissist's victim never abandons him.

By coming on hard at first, the narcissist fosters emotions of reliance on the victim. This is known as "love bombing." It's the stuff of lousy romance novels, and it's one of narcissism's most egregious manifestations. The narcissist is the only one who loves the victim as much as the victim loves the narcissist. Indeed, narcissists pay their victims' such close attention that they think that no one will ever love them as much as their narcissists do. Because love bombing produces such a high, the victim develops a strong desire for it. For the narcissist, however, this step is simply part of the valuing and then depreciating phase. In essence, the narcissist places others on a pedestal at first. The narcissist's attention target can't go wrong.

However, things swiftly turn nasty. The narcissist's dread of being never abandoned truly goes away. The narcissist gradually devalues the target of their adoration. The narcissist is attempting to reduce the impacts of the desertion that the narcissist feels is on the horizon by doing so. To avoid being abandoned by the victim, the narcissist may end their relationship with the victim.

On the other hand, the victim can turn the situation around by breaking up with the narcissist. This act revs up the narcissist's engine. More lovebombing happens to keep the victim in the narcissist's grip.

The narcissist may lash out at the victim for breaking up with them in the most extreme circumstances. The narcissist may then embark on a campaign to harm the victim's reputation or attempt to steal the victim's friends. Physical violence might occur in the worst-case situation when the victim quits the narcissist because the narcissist would not let anybody leave. At least briefly, physical violence or the prospect of it frequently puts a halt to the abandoning.

9. The Narcissist Lives in a Fantasy

Because narcissists frequently have illusions of grandeur, they will conjure up grandiose illusions about their illustrious lives. It's delusions that the narcissist wants others to join in on and validate as genuine. The narcissist's fantasies are diverse. According to the narcissist, they are more attractive and talented than anybody else and brighter, wealthier, and more powerful.

To justify their fantasies, narcissists frequently fabricate stories about events that never occurred, or, if an event did occur, they alter the facts to make it appear larger, better, or brighter than it actually was. Governors, millionaires, and movie stars are all part of the narcissist's universe. Thousands of adoring devotees prostrate themselves at their feet. When or if someone points out that the fantasy is a falsehood, the narcissist goes on a rant. This stems from a desire to safeguard the narcissist's long-forgotten fake self.

While their behavior frequently causes harm to those around them, the actual harm began when the narcissists first suffered their narcissistic wound. In order to survive whatever trauma the narcissist endured, they were obliged to develop a new, more acceptable self. The narcissist's fantasy world supports this fake persona. The narcissist's phony self will shatter if the fantasy's support erodes. Of course, this isn't an excuse for the narcissist's frequently bad behavior. It does, however, explain why the narcissist's illusion is so vital to him.

10. There Are Always Strings Attached

Victims who have learned the narcissist's tricks realize that no gift comes without conditions. The ignorant must learn this lesson the hard way. Unexpected gifts from the narcissist are later used to persuade the victim to do what the narcissist desires. The narcissist never provides a gift only to give. Gifts are given with the expectation of receiving something in return, whether real or immaterial. The narcissist always ensures that the recipient is aware that the present is from him. There is often an implicit understanding with the narcissist that the narcissist would collect at a later date.

It's even better if the individual getting the message is in a bad mood. The narcissist has the ability to save this helpless victim. The receiver, in turn, pays and pays and pays. The narcissist provides to cultivate loyalty, ensuring that no one ever abandons him. The narcissist may sometimes provide so much that it makes some individuals reliant on the narcissist. This is advantageous to the narcissist since it ensures that they have various sources of narcissistic supply at all times.

Unfortunately for the sufferer of this narcissistic strategy, accepting presents from anybody becomes impossible. The dread that such presents are attached to strings is always there in the victim's thoughts. This makes it difficult for the narcissist's victims to trust other people's intentions, even if those intentions are genuine.

Concluding Thoughts on Characteristics of Narcissism

Despite its status as a recognized psychological disease, there are still many unknowns and doubts surrounding it. Unfortunately, people with NPD are frequently protective about their personalities and reject intervention or therapy. Nonetheless, understanding narcissism symptoms is the first step toward resolving an unpleasant and potentially life-altering illness.

Those who are affected by the narcissist's actions must also make an effort to lessen the harm caused by the narcissist. First and foremost, people who a narcissist has harmed must establish boundaries. By their very nature, narcissists take advantage of others because they have no empathy for their suffering. They will go to any length to fulfill their desires, even if it means using nefarious methods. Therefore, those around them must set firm and obvious limits and be prepared to enforce them if they are to survive.

Second, the narcissist's victims should understand that the narcissist's actions never indicate the victims' worthiness. While the narcissist may dish out the abuse that appears to be directed at you, it isn't. Instead, it is the result of the narcissist's profound sense of inadequacy. This isn't to mean that the narcissist's mistreated the individual shouldn't fight back. This activity, however, should come from a place of self-care.

Finally, self-care may imply avoiding the narcissist. Limiting a person's exposure to the narcissist might be adequate in some cases. However, the individual who the narcissist has abused may have decided not to visit the narcissist any longer. For someone who understands the traits of narcissism, walking away becomes a bit easier: the individual who fully understands what the narcissist is about recognizes the indicators as the warnings they are.

How Our Personalities Change After Narcissistic Abuse

The ramifications of narcissistic abuse may be far-reaching and long-lasting, whether you are a victim for a few weeks or a few years. Our sense of self is destroyed by narcissistic abuse, and it may also damage our personality. We alter due to narcissism's misery and instability, and we change who we are to endure its devastating repercussions.

Bottomed-Out Confidence

Perhaps the most damaging consequence of narcissistic abuse on our personalities is the resulting loss of confidence. Narcissists must damage our trust to undermine any questions we may ask and any limits we could establish. You can see through a narcissist's flimsy tactics when you know your value, and you can stand up for yourself and the things you need when you know your value. The narcissist abuser can't stand it because they need total control over their relationships, friends, and even family.

Constant Internalization

Do you have a constant sense of blame on your shoulders? That tendency of focusing on the issues of the world rather than your own? This isn't a haphazard pattern. It's frequently caused by narcissistic abuse. It might be the effect of narcissistic abuse if your formerly powerful personality has become heavy with blame and an almost incomprehensible sense of worthlessness. Narcissists make us assume responsibility for their faults as well as life's unavoidable calamities. This, along with our loss of confidence, results in a person continuously sacrificing themselves on the altar of internalized blame over time.

Post-Traumatic Stress Disorder (PTSD)

Some people believe that PTSD affects only warriors or those who have experienced severe physical trauma, yet this could not be further from reality. When we are involved in an encounter or incident that significantly and fundamentally destabilizes who we are or what we believe, we may develop Post-Traumatic Stress Disorder. Unfortunately, narcissistic abuse accomplishes precisely that, and the aftermath may leave us feeling bewildered and drained.

Insecure Attachment

Because narcissistic abuse is so disruptive, it influences our ability to connect and attach to people, which may significantly influence who we are and how we approach our lives and relationships. For example, when we discover that it isn't safe to love or open up to someone, we either avoid it, get concerned about it, or utilize a mixture of the two, our relationships become explosive and explosive. The longer you are subjected to this form of abuse, the more warped and scared your worldview will become, dramatically altering your viewpoint and personality.

Even More Narcissism

Unfortunately, living and loving in the shadow of a narcissist might lead to our own narcissistic traits. Humans are social beings who seek to imitate what we perceive to be "normal" conduct. The longer you live in a society of narcissistic devaluation, the more likely you are to assume that this is a normal and acceptable way of life and interaction. As a result, you may begin to show narcissistic characteristics of your own, as well as a lack of empathy and sympathy for others.

Superficiality

Living with or loving a narcissist necessitates a certain level of superficiality, which may seep into our personality. You can't be honest or transparent about how you're feeling with narcissists. You must act to be pleased and involved, even if you don't mean it, or you risk being rejected. Unfortunately, this becomes the norm, and you carry it out in your daily life, feigning feelings you don't have and putting up with people and things you despise or disagree with.

Crippled Communication Skills

You may find it challenging to open up and interact with others as openly or successfully as you did before your relationship with a narcissist, even if you were previously a gregarious or outgoing person because it's not safe to express yourself as a victim of narcissistic abuse or to open up and discuss what you're experiencing or what's essential to you. It wreaks havoc on your communication abilities, which in turn wreaks havoc on your friendships, attitude, and whole attitude.

The Most Effective Ways To Rebuild Yourself After Narcissistic Abuse

These are the best strategies to rebuild yourself and your future in the aftermath of narcissistic abuse, whether you decide to continue with your spouse or have already called it quits and emancipated yourself from the narcissist in your life.

1. Arm Yourself With Understanding

Understanding and awareness are two of the most powerful tools we have in the fight against narcissistic abuse and the long-term consequences it leaves behind. The more we learn how narcissists operate, the more we will be able to see the harm they have caused in our own lives. Then, with this new understanding in hand, we can devise a strategy to repair the harm and reclaim our complete selves.

Find out as much as you can about narcissists and how they operate. Don't be hesitant to draw parallels where they're necessary, and don't be hesitant to recognize yourself in the victims and the terrible consequences of abuse.

The more you learn, the more you'll understand yourself and how you've responded to the abuse you've experienced. You'll be able to see what parts of your personality have slunk away in shame, and what needs to be clawed back and what needs to be let go. Don't be afraid to tell it how it is. Don't be scared to be completely honest with yourself, as well as with your spouse. Once you've grasped and accepted what's going on, you may take steps to correct it.

2. Know Your Worth

Knowing our value has a profound effect on our willingness to compromise on important issues. We, like everyone else, have a right to happiness and power in this world. Relationships are about constructing something together, not about subjecting one another. When you understand the worth of what you offer to the table, you will refuse to let those vital parts of yourself be torn away or denied in any manner.

Begin to accept that you are just as valuable and deserving as anybody else on the earth. You are deserving of love. You are deserving of respect. When you work hard and consistently for your goals, you deserve to have them. Make this understanding the cornerstone of all you do by using it to stand up for the things that matter to you.

"I am entitled to this." Say that three times a day to yourself and believe it. Stop allowing others to usurp the space you were born to occupy and begin to value the sanctity of your own existence. Don't think of things in terms of them vs you, and remember that you are solely accountable for your own journey. When you understand your value, you'll quit putting up with terrible conduct and restricting partners that take away from who you are. You'll make sure you obtain it once you realize you have just as much right to happiness as everyone else.

3. Lean Into Boundaries

Boundaries are amazing things that help us protect our health and define our relationships in more steady and efficient ways. When you use your boundaries to reconfirm who you are and what you want, it's simpler for others around you to grasp what's expected of them. You also make it easy for yourself to articulate your demands and the rest of the world to understand the boundaries and why they are there. If you want to understand how to defend yourself against future narcissistic intrusions, lean into your limits.

Your boundaries are wonderful. They should be honored. If you don't know what they are, start spending time alone with yourself on a regular basis and consider what can help you define them. Ask yourself probing questions such as, "How do I expect to be treated?" and "What kind of person can't I have in my space?" These responses might help you figure out what is important to you and what doesn't.

Spend as much time as necessary familiarizing yourself with your boundary lines, but don't stop there. However, the most crucial aspect of leaning into your limits is not just establishing them. It's about figuring out how to follow through on them. If you declare anything a "no-go" zone, ensure the repercussions are activated when the boundary is crossed. That's what it entails, rather than ending your relationship or simply a particular portion of it. Stop allowing yourself to be bulldozed or otherwise cornered when it comes to your limits.

4. Embrace Your Uniqueness (And Who You Want To Be)

Learning to enjoy who you are is a terrific approach to get back on track to who you are. Because this instability makes it simpler for narcissists to maintain control, they push us away from our authenticity. We reclaim our power and eliminate control from someone who might otherwise disparage our attractiveness when we not only accept but enjoy who we are. Learn to celebrate who you want to be and how to do so. Stop letting other people's opinions influence what you know you're supposed to do.

Consider your advantages. Take into account your flaws as well. Take a look at each of them side by side to get a sense of the overall picture they generate. Some of your strengths may already be celebrated, but you must also learn to enjoy your flaws. Allowing a narcissist to belittle you should not prevent you from recognizing the silver lining in things you may otherwise dismiss as flaws.

Celebrate who you are now, but be in the habit of looking ahead to your future self. Consider who you want to be in ten or twenty years. Concentrate on that image and use it to motivate yourself to leave the narcissistic abuse route. Every time you take a step toward becoming that person, acknowledge the progress you've achieved. Don't minimize your accomplishments, no matter how minor they may look. Any progressive progress (away from a narcissist) is a step in the right direction. Get in the habit of appreciating who you are and the efforts you take toward being the person you've always wanted to be.

5. Tap Into Your Support Networks

In the fight to reclaim our identities, our support networks may be vital. We see a wider and more full image of the worth we provide to the world via our friends, family, and loved ones. They frequently see us in the finest light when we only see the negative, and they often recognize strengths that we are unwilling to acknowledge amid belittlement and grief. If you want to go back to who you are, tap into your support networks and allow them to be the guiding light back to your personality.

Make contact with the people who are most important to you. Open up about your experiences and let them know where you're at emotionally right now. Allow your support networks to do what they were created to do: help. Don't be scared to show them who you truly are by letting them sec you as you think you are.

When we open up to our loved ones, we can regain our confidence and find inspiration (and motivation) to break out from the narcissistic abuse that is killing our sense of self. Allow no long separations or difficult internalizations to prevent you from reaching out to the ones who are most eager to assist you. Lean on your support networks and ask for their help when you don't feel like going on. There is no shame in seeking comfort or assistance from others.

6. Fall In Love With Yourself

No one on this earth can love you as deeply as you can love yourself. That's because you're the only one who has witnessed every event you've ever had and knows all there is to know about yourself. You are the one person who will ever witness the whole spectrum of your abilities and flaws and then remain with you in the end despite or in spite of them. When you love yourself, you learn to love others — and you learn to defeat those who want to keep you from being who you are.

Spend some time getting to know yourself (again or for the first time). Then, create a daily "you time" regimen that allows you to spend one-on-one time with this body and this person with whom you will spend the rest of your life.

Examine your assets. Take pleasure in them. Recognize the importance they provide to your life and the chances they've provided. Consider how they help you become a more distinct and well-rounded individual. Then devote some time to your flaws and pay attention to the things they have to offer you.

You learn to fall in love with both when you learn to fall in love with yourself. Finally, let go of the mistakes, hang on to the lessons, and remember that your experiences do not define you. Your response to them defines who you are.

Why Narcissists Act The Way They Do

You might be smitten by their lovely aspect while being destroyed by their sinister side. It's perplexing at first, but once you grasp what motivates them, it all makes sense. Moreover, this knowledge shields you from their ruses, falsehoods, and deception.

Narcissists have an underdeveloped or defective self. They think and act in a different way than most others. They act the way they do because of the way their brain is built, which can be inherited or learned. Narcissism can be mild or severe. Some narcissists have a greater number of symptoms with a higher severity, while others have fewer, milder symptoms. As a result, the following explanation may not apply equally to all narcissists.

Narcissistic Vulnerability

Despite their intimidating personas, narcissists are quite susceptible. They are considered "fragile" by psychotherapists.

They experience deep alienation, emptiness, impotence, and a sense of meaninglessness. They desire power due to their great fragility, and they must constantly monitor their environment, the people around them, and their moods. Fear, guilt, or despair, for example, are unbearable signals of weakness in oneself and others. Their defensive mechanism, which is detailed farther below, protects them but harms others. When they're feeling insecure, they're more spiteful, and the consequences of their acts don't matter.

Narcissistic Shame

Toxic shame, which may or may not be conscious, lies beneath their exterior. Narcissists are made to feel insecure and inadequate by shame, which they must deny to themselves and others. This is one reason that they can't take criticism, responsibility, dissent, or negative feedback even when meant to be constructive. Instead, they want others' absolute favorable respect.

Arrogance

They cultivate a superior demeanor to compensate for their feelings of inferiority. They're frequently arrogant, critical, and dismissive of others, especially whole groups they consider inferior, such as immigrants, members of a racial minority, those from a lower socioeconomic status, and those with less education. They, like bullies, cast others down in order to elevate themselves.

Grandiosity

Their braggadocio and self-aggrandizement are due to their underlying humiliation. They're trying to persuade themselves and others that they're exceptional, that they're the best, smartest, wealthiest, most attractive, and talented people on the planet. This is also why narcissists prefer celebrities and high-status individuals and schools, companies, and other institutions. Being around the best convinces them that they are superior to others, despite their own doubts.

Entitlement

Narcissists believe they have the right to acquire anything they desire from others, regardless of their actions. Their feeling of entitlement hides their humiliation and insecurity on the inside. They persuade themselves that they are superior, and as a result, they are entitled to preferential treatment. Their time is more precious than others'. Thus they shouldn't have to queue like the rest of us. What they could demand from others has no bounds. Because other individuals are deemed inferior and not separate from them, interpersonal connections are one-way streets. They don't see their actions as hypocritical since they believe they are better and unique. Therefore, they are exempt from the rules that apply to others.

Lack of Empathy

The ability of narcissists to act emotionally and exhibit adequate care and concern is severely hampered. Narcissists lack empathy, according to the Diagnostic and Statistical Manual of Mental Disorders. They're "unwilling to understand or sympathize with other people's feelings or needs." 2013 (APA) They exhibit structural anomalies in brain areas related to emotional empathy, according to research.

They may pretend to love you, but the way they treat you will decide whether you feel loved. True love needs empathy, compassion, and a thorough understanding of the person we love. We demonstrate an active interest in that person's life and development. We strive to grasp their perspective and experience, even if it differs from ours. If you haven't experienced genuine love, or if it has been combined with abuse, you may not be able to appreciate it or expect to be treated better.

When it isn't in their best interests to be charming or cooperative, narcissists may be selfish, cruel, and frigid. Relationships are transactional to them. They're more focused on having their demands filled than on responding to feelings, even if it involves abusing others, cheating, lying, or violating the law. They may experience excitement and passion in the early stages of a relationship, but this is desire, not love. They're famed for their ability to play games. It's not in their game plan to make a sacrifice for a loved one. Their lack of empathy makes them immune to the suffering they inflict on others. Still, their cognitive and emotional competence provides them with an advantage in manipulating and using others to meet their wants.

Emptiness

Narcissists struggle to emotionally connect with people because they lack a good emotional connection to themselves. Because of their underdeveloped ego and limited inner resources, they must rely on others for affirmation. Rather than confidence, they are afraid of becoming unpopular. They can only admire themselves when they see themselves reflected in other people's eyes. As a result, despite their bragging and self-flattery, they seek continual attention and praise. They strive to control what others think of them to feel better about themselves since their sense of self is dictated by what others think of them. Relationships are a source of self-enhancement and narcissistic supply for them. They are never content, though, because of their inner emptiness. Whatever you do for them never seems to be enough to fill their void. Narcissists abuse and drain everyone around them, much like vampires who are dead inside.

Lack of Boundaries

Mythological stories Narcissus was enchanted by his own reflection in a pool of water. He didn't know it was himself at first. Narcissists are symbolically described in this way. Because of their inner emptiness, guilt, and underdeveloped ego, narcissists are unsure of their boundaries. Because narcissists are unable to empathize, they see other people as two-dimensional extensions of themselves without empathy. Other individuals exist just to serve their wants. This explains why, even when harsh, narcissists are selfish and blind to their influence on others.

Narcissistic Defenses

Relationships with narcissists are challenging because of their defensive measures to shield their vulnerability. Arrogance and scorn, denial, projection, violence, and jealousy are all common defenses they employ.

Arrogance and contempt

These defenses enhance a narcissist's ego with an aura of superiority to protect against unconscious thoughts of inadequacy. By projecting inadequacy onto others, it also redirects shame.

Denial

Denial distorts reality so that a narcissist may preserve their fragile ego by living in an inflated bubble of their own fantasy world. They distort, justify, twist facts, and deceive themselves to avoid anything that could cause a breach in their armor, which is so thick that no amount of proof or argument can break through to certain narcissists.

Projection and blame

This protection allows unpleasant feelings, emotions, or attributes to be discarded and assigned to someone else mentally or vocally. The narcissist is blameless because blaming transfers responsibility. This response is similar to denial in that it serves the same purpose. Projection is an unconscious technique in which a narcissist does not have to experience anything terrible in themselves because they perceive it to be external. Instead, such characteristics are projected onto someone else or a group of individuals. As a result, you become a selfish, weak, unlovable, or useless person. Projection may drive those close to a narcissist insane and harm their self-esteem, especially children.

Aggression

By pushing individuals away, aggression is employed to create a sense of safety. Narcissists perceive the world as hostile and scary, and they use violent language and conduct to attack others. This may escalate to narcissistic abuse. By overcoming their perpetrator, vindictive narcissists are able to reverse emotions of shame and reclaim their dignity.

Envy

Narcissists must be the greatest in the world. They are unable to take joy in the achievement of others. It makes people feel inferior when someone else has what they want. It's a zero-sum game in life. Competitive narcissists are not just envious of others who have what they desire; they may retaliate vengefully in order to pull them down, especially if they feel threatened. With their offspring, narcissists are frequently jealous and competitive.

Impacts Of Growing Up With A Narcissistic Parent

The notion that "I am not good enough" is formed due to being raised by a narcissistic parent.

Narcissistic parents are typically possessive of their young children. Their children are viewed as an extension of themselves, and they become a source of self-esteem for the parent: "Look at how perfect my children are. Didn't I do a fantastic job?" In addition, the youngsters are used as a technique of attracting people's attention.

Children learn to fit into the molds that their parents build for them, which may cause anxiety in the kid who is continually putting their own identity on the back burner to satisfy the parent.

For their life to be secure, the kid of a narcissistic parent must follow the parent's agenda. When children assert their feelings or opinions, it can lead to conflicts with their parents, such as rage, tears, or punishment. The youngster learns that their feelings and thoughts are meaningless, invalid, and insignificant due to this and will frequently suppress their own emotions to preserve the peace at home.

Narcissists aren't always as harsh as they appear. They can be quite nice, but their charity nearly always comes with strings attached. The youngster will frequently come to realize that their parent's goodwill makes them feel obligated to them. The sentiment "If I do this for you, you owe me" always comes with acts of kindness, whether overt or covert. Love and kindness are both conditional.

At the best of times, a narcissist's behavior can be challenging to deal with, but it can feel extremely unpredictable and unsettling for a child. Because young children cannot simply rise and leave their families, they cultivate hope by sacrificing their own self-esteem and condemning themselves. "If I were better at this or that, my parent would love me more," the youngster internalizes the concept that they are the issue. The parent's own opinion that they are the perfect parent only adds to this notion since they assume that any resistance or negativity from the kid is due to the kid.

Growing up with a narcissistic parent is challenging since the youngster is frequently unaware that anything is wrong. We only know what our family exposes us to when we are growing up. Years later, the kid, who is frequently already an adult, attempts to make meaning of their childhood. This realization is frequently facilitated by a friend or spouse who can recognize the narcissist's unique or strange parenting.

Traits of Adult Children of a Narcissistic Parent

1. Indecision and Guilt

Adult offspring of narcissistic parents are afraid that doing what is good for them would harm someone else. They have been "trained to prioritize their parents" demands, making it difficult for them to prioritize their own needs without seeming selfish. For years, indecision and remorse may paralyze you.

2. Internalized Gaslighting

Gaslighting is a type of psychological manipulation in which a person or a group subtly sows seeds of doubt in a target individual's memory, perception, or judgment.

Growing up with a narcissistic parent can make an adult kid feel as if they have nothing to give, even if this is not the case. Growing up, the narcissistic parent who felt threatened by their child's abilities may have minimized, neglected, or co-opted their talents and capabilities.

Even if the now-adult achieves success, they may believe they did not earn it, leading to impostor syndrome.

3) Love and Loyalty

Adult offspring of narcissists may find it difficult to separate themselves from their narcissistic parent, even after growing up surrounded by lies, manipulation, and abuse. They will most likely feel guilty for attempting to pull back or set boundaries, and they may even pursue relationships with narcissistic people.

They are used to love based on manipulations and restrictions, yet pure love may be frightening.

4) Strength and Resilience

Adult offspring of narcissistic parents frequently have a high level of compassion and love for others and the capacity to develop loving relationships and learn to love and care for themselves. Growing up with a narcissistic parent can be difficult, but it is possible to rehabilitate, as will be explored later in this chapter.

5) Chronic Self-blame

Whether the parent is publicly abusive to their kid or not, they are nearly always emotionally tone-deaf, too absorbed with themselves and their own issues to hear their child's misery. As previously said, in order to keep the family unit together, the kid (even if they are now an adult) avoids criticizing their parents and instead places all of the responsibility on themselves: "If I was better at...", "If I wasn't such a difficult child...", and so on.

This can even continue into adulthood, with the adult kid taking responsibility for things that aren't necessarily their fault.

Unfortunately, in many circumstances, they are made the scapegoat just to preserve the peace.

6) Echoism

Echoists and Narcissists complement each other, and you can read more about Echoism here. Essentially, narcissistic parents can explode into anger or burst into tears without much warning, forcing their children to take up as little space as possible to avoid triggering one of these emotional outbursts. It can feel like walking on eggshells, trying to do everything possible to avoid their parent having a meltdown.

7) Insecure Attachment

Adult offspring of narcissists are more prone to develop insecure attachments to their parents, never having had the safe basis that they require to feel comfortable exploring their surroundings.

A parent's neglect, manipulation, or emotional absence might cause a youngster to wonder how secure they would feel in other people's hands. Some adults become fiercely independent due to this, believing that no one else can be trusted. On the other hand, others may feel compelled to cling to their relationships for affection and demand their significant other's undivided attention at all times.

8) Parentified Child

Children with a narcissistic parent will have built their entire life and personality on their parent's happiness. They will then grow up to make their lives around the happiness of others, with many of them working in helping professions.

How You Can Move Forwards

You may go ahead and heal from being raised by a narcissistic parent in a variety of ways. However, I would not advise you to try to accomplish this alone; it is up to you whether you engage in a therapy partnership or work through your recovery with a partner. Working through this healing process with a family member might lead to complications, so approach with caution.

Here are some essential things to take to start the healing process:

1) Recognize.

The first step, like with anything, is to become conscious. We can't move on unless we figure out what's causing us pain. If you're reading this chapter, it's likely that one of your parents had a narcissistic personality disorder or had narcissistic features.

2) Study

Learn as much as you can about NPD and the effects it may have on the family structure. Examine the internet, study textbooks, and speak with therapists who are familiar with narcissism.

3) Recount your experiences

Because this activity might be challenging, I strongly advise that you get assistance. Recall and put down your personal experiences from infancy or adulthood that fit each indication and symptom of NPD.

The narrative for each of these memories has to be rewritten with a new dialogue that says, "My parent is a narcissist, and he/she is treating me this way because of it." This new conversation has no guilt, neither for you nor for your parent. Instead, this is a technique for re-framing your experiences in light of fresh facts and absolving yourself of responsibility.

4) Identify

It's quite likely that the narcissistic parent's abusive, traumatic, and inattentive behavior will be revealed during the preceding phase. You will almost certainly be able to detect emotional abuse and neglect (guilt-tripping, manipulating), as well as psychological abuse, as terrible as it may be (gaslighting or the silent treatment). You may also come across incidents of physical and financial abuse (neglect or excessive gift-giving). Working with these experiences with a counselor may be tremendously beneficial.

5) Grieve

In this sort of healing, there might be a lot of mourning. You're mourning both for the upbringing you didn't have and for the picture of your parent that has been broken. As previously said, we only know what we know as children. When a result, as you become older and realize that other children had a vastly different upbringing than you, you may feel envious, betrayed, or furious that you didn't get to experience it.

You may have grown up idolizing or protecting your parents, only to discover that they have really harmed you. This may be quite destabilizing, and we may discover that we need to grieve for the picture of our parents that we used to have.

6) Work through developmental milestones.

You probably missed some critical developmental stages as a child, and now is the time to start experiencing and learning about them. Now is the time to figure out who you are, to play about with your sexuality, to date, to figure out what you want to study and what you truly want to accomplish with your life. You'll almost certainly have to learn to ask for what you need (you may start simple, like asking for directions), recognize your suppressed emotions, and create appropriate limits.

7) Understand.

Finally, it's critical to recognize and accept that your narcissistic parent is unlikely to change. No matter how much you want to face them or how much you face them, the parent is unlikely to modify their habits.

Confronting a narcissistic parent may lead to significant family strife because, as previously said, a narcissist will experience enormous humiliation and vulnerability when their immaculate image is pierced. This might cause them to become irritated and defensive.

It's also crucial to recognize and maybe forgive your other parent. If one of your parents is a narcissist, the other is almost certainly an enabler. Enablers effectively normalize and maintain the narcissist's abusive behavior by going along with and/or justifying it. Enablers can go along with the narcissist's dirty work, tolerating and sustaining their abuse. Enablers become complicit when they don't name the abuse and protect their children from it, even if they are victims as well.

The Signs That You Have a Narcissistic Mother

While narcissistic parents do share some common traits, some characteristics are more common in mothers or fathers. Narcissistic mothers employ drastic back and forth methods that result in psychological and emotional whiplash for their children. This back and forth is mostly due to how a narcissistic mother presents herself to other people versus how she is at home. She can be charismatic, friendly, and personable in public, but critical, insulting, and controlling at home.

Narcissistic mothers are often outwardly friendly. They portray an air of confidence, success and act as if everything in their life is seamless and perfect. Whatever they do looks comfortable: working sixty hours a week, owning a lavish home, being on the PTA, and appearing involved in their kids' lives.

Narcissistic mothers appear to be able to do it all and make it look so simple!

Their friends, colleagues, and other parents adore them and might even feel envious of how simple and perfect a narcissistic mother makes her life look.

The only problem is, it is all an image, an inflated self-image that isn't anywhere close to what a narcissistic mom is genuinely like. At home, a child raised by a narcissistic mother knows the difference. Mom is controlling, critical, angry, and demanding. That face of perfect happiness and constant ease goes away. She uses an abusive tactic of withholding to make her children compliant, dependent, and insecure, all while forcing them to show her gratitude and praise.

It is worth noting that success does not mean narcissism. Most career oriented, financially successful women are not narcissists. Extroverted and involved moms are also not automatically narcissists. These traits are common in a narcissistic mother, but they are not defining. The significant differences between healthy moms and narcissistic moms are seen in how they are at home.

When a narcissistic mom comes home, she will want to control her children and micromanage them. A healthy mother comes home to support and nurture her children. When they are at home, narcissistic mothers continue to need and demand gratitude, affection, and attention, even at the expense of their children's needs. Narcissistic mothers lack empathy towards their children and are angered by any kind of independence that their children may try to gain for themselves. A narcissistic mother is always right because she has to be correct.

When the socially engaged, publicly adored narcissistic mother comes home, her smile fades. She diverges from that "perfect" image and becomes controlling, manipulative, and demeaning towards her children, as well as a romantic partner if there is one in the picture. This shift can be very confusing to adolescents and isn't entirely understood until adulthood in most cases.

Narcissistic mothers rely heavily on manipulation for control. They expect you to do what they want when they want, and if you do not, they will insult, belittle, and degrade you. Any time you are not fulfilling mom's needs or doing whatever she wants to make her think her needs are of the utmost importance, her attacks will come in the form of vicious criticism.

One of a narcissistic mom's favorite manipulative lines can sound a lot like,

"If you loved me, you would do what I want. If you do not do it, you do not love me." She is easily offended and will resort to guilt if she does not get what she wants. Accusations of not loving her, not valuing her, or taking her for granted will be used frequently.

Since a narcissistic mom has an image to keep up, you might see her being friendly and accepting in public. Then, when you get home, you will hear everything she has to say that is negative about a person she was smiling with and agreeing with earlier that day. Mom is opinionated, but not at the expense of her superficial image.

Narcissistic mothers are going to find faults and negativities in anything you do that does not please them. They will demean and insult you, and even when you go to great lengths to make it right, you will never get recognition for that. Apologies mean nothing and are never going to be enough. Actions to make up for what you did wrong in your mother's eyes are not going to be adequate either.

Everyone enjoys praise and validation on some level. Children are no exception. However, since narcissistic mothers lack empathy, you won't be getting recognition from them. If anything, she will minimize your accomplishments or achievements unless they directly fluff up her ego. She will make you feel anxious about her lack of praise and constant marginalization of what you do.

If a narcissistic mother raised you, you know that mom needs to be the center of attention at all times. She will expect you to love her, adore her, shower her with praise, take care of her, and wait on her and all her needs.

She never returns any of these sentiments or favors because she is the only one that matters to her. This expectation is entirely one-sided, which can lead to resentment and feelings of low self-esteem and lack of confidence in children. Always feeling like they do not matter makes them think they do not matter. Narcissistic mothers are great at making their children feel like they do not matter.

The crux of the situation is that every human is biologically programmed to want and seek maternal affection. A child raised by a narcissistic mother who is deprived of that affection or is given praise and appreciation on a conditional basis will develop a lot of emotional and mental problems that extend into adulthood. Most children who discover that they were raised by a narcissistic mother continue to seek her approval and affection, even knowing on some level that she cannot give it.

Narcissistic mothers are master manipulators in playing on the emotions, vulnerabilities, and insecurities of their children. It becomes normalized in the family dynamic. Narcissistic mothers also use emotional manipulation to play family members against each other to remain the focal point of attention and the one who receives the most love and affection. Siblings fight; they confide in mom and offer her their love while harboring resentment for their siblings. If siblings or a child and father attempt to form a closer bond, narcissistic mothers can get jealous and further damage that relationship. Narcissistic mothers rely heavily on emotional manipulation for control. They seek adoration and validation from within the home and from external sources as well.

The Flashy Extrovert

The extrovert mother is one of the most common kinds of narcissistic mothers you will find around. In the public's eyes, they are entirely perfect, and everyone wants to be like them. Outside, she is fun, easy to notice, and very flashy. If her child can keep up the act out, the better the treatment meted to him or her. If the child can't, he or she will be treated with a cold shoulder.

Only those who live with her know that she is not who she portrays herself to be. Her children will most likely have no love for her because they know she is a pretender. She gives love to only those who can help her keep up her appearances in the external world. Everyone, including strangers, loves these kinds of narcissistic mothers, except her children, which makes them desperately yearn for her love. In most cases, these mothers have a great social circle that they want to keep intact. For this reason, they force their children to do all they can to fit in by projecting what she wants through them.

The Accomplishment-Oriented Mothers

To this group of narcissistic mothers, your achievement in life is her utmost priority. She expects her children to perform their best using the standards she has put in place. Her definition of success and achievement is based on what a person does and not who they are. If you want the love of this kind of mother, your grades have to be the best; you need to be the top at every game and tournament, get admission to the leading colleges, and get a job with the most prestigious organizations.

These mothers enjoy getting attention by using the accomplishment of their kids. If you meet up to her standards, you will be showered with love and affection at every turn. However, if you fail to meet these standards and fall in the process of reaching them, it embarrasses her. Children who do this are satisfied with her wrath and fury.

It can be very confusing dealing with this mother because you have no support when you put all of the work involved in meeting her standards. However, the instant you can meet her expectations, you become the apple of her eye.

She all smiles when she attends the award ceremonies that happen as a result of your achievements. Children with this type of narcissistic mother soon understand that if they want the attention, love, and support of their mother, they have to be at the top. This may lead the child into a high-achieving lifestyle. Besides, they are usually devastated if they fail because they know what comes next.

The Psychosomatic Mothers

This group of mothers enjoys manipulating their children, and they use aches, illnesses, and pains to do it. She uses all of these tools to ensure attention stays on her at all times. She needs to prioritize others, and any child who wants the love and attention of this mother has to play the role of a caretaker.

If you call her out on her behavior or fail to fall for her antics, she gets into a health crisis. This usually works in making you feel guilty for failing to be there when your mother needed you the most.

The only important thing to a mother is for her child to be at her beck, caring for her. This strategy is also useful for the mother in getting away from difficult situations. If she hears something terrible that she doesn't want to deal with, feigning a particular illness is her next option. If you listened to this phrase; "Don't break the news to your mother, or her sickness will worsen," then you may have been dealing with a psychosomatic mother.

In addition to caring for her, another way to get attention from this mother is to fall sick. This is something many children find out later on. The reason for this is that being sick makes them connect on mutual ground. However, if the child's sickness is worse than that of the mother and ends up taking up all of the attention, the mother will not be pleased with it. She feels entitled to all the care and won't be happy when her child takes it all.

The Addicted Narcissistic Mother

These narcissistic mothers deal with substance abuse. However, their behavior is more prominent whenever they are under the influence of any substance they are addicted to. Anytime the effect of the importance wears off, they portray fewer narcissistic behaviors. But sometimes, this is not the case.

To these mothers, they prioritize the substance. Nobody else matters until they satisfy their addiction. They must cater to their addiction before they do anything else.

The Subtly Abusive

These mothers share some similarities with extrovert mothers. They are very particular about how those on the outside see them and would prefer if no one outside was aware of her abuses at home. These mothers usually have a personality they display in private and a different one in public.

On the outside, they are the kindest, sweetest, loving, and most sensitive mother, any child, can have. However, when they are home, they become mean and abusive. For children who live with these types of mothers, their lives can be confusing.

Also, this mother can say one thing in public and say something entirely different in private. For instance, when in public, she could announce to everyone how proud she is of her child in a room. But in private, she will continuously tell her child how much of a disappointment they are. This kind of inconsistent behavior can be very confusing for the child and can lead to a long-term ripple effect.

The Emotionally Needy

Most narcissistic mothers have this trait. However, those mothers in this category make it more prominent than others. They dump all of their emotional baggage on their children and expect them to listen, care for, and understand them. In an ideal family, this is supposed to be the other way around. In time, the children begin to play the roles of therapists trying to solve problems they should not have any business solving in the first place.

While this is going on, the children's emotional needs are ignored, and even when they do garner the courage to ask their mother for help, the help they get from her is almost insignificant. If it is not about her, then it is not essential.

The Flamboyant Extroverted Mother

This one is the ideal mother for everyone out there. She is loved by everyone, neighbors, friends, and even random strangers because she is adorable and friendly. She has it all going in the public eye, and she continually strives to maintain that image. She will be offended by anyone or anything that might seem to change this perception. However, she secretly is a monster in her home to the children. She will control them and be mean to them, but still ensuring that whatever they do in the public eye always makes her look like the best mother in the world. The children fear her and cannot seek help as they feel like there is no way out, and no one would believe them anyway.

The Addict

Substance abuse always ends up turning people into something they should not be. Mothers who abuse drugs or are alcoholics always tend to be narcissistic as the addiction controls their emotions and everything they do. They also always choose substance over family; hence, a misunderstanding comes up, and they will run to the bottle and blame it later. They do not take responsibility for anything, and when cornered, they will always abuse. When high due to addiction, most of them tend to vent all the anger and pain of the children. A few times, they are good mothers when they are sober, but it only lasts for a short while. They will also get high and always blame their children for the addiction.

The Mean Mother

This one is mean to her children, and she will not want her children to have what she cannot have or never had. She will continuously interfere in the good things that the children might have, so she can always be the one looking good or being praised. She will not let the daughter have the right car if she doesn't have one. She will not allow the son to have a lovely house if she has not built one for her. This limits her children so much, as they cannot make any better life than hers. The children end up doing things in secret so they can enjoy some luxuries without her knowledge.

The Success-Oriented Mother

This one is only concerned about what the children accomplish and nothing else. She will continuously compare her children with their peers if they look like they have more accomplishments than her children. She is always happy when her children get luxurious things, especially if she knows she can benefit from them. She is glad to visit her children in big homes, be driven around in big cars, and boast of how successful her family is. Anyone that is not successful in her family will continuously be intimidated and ignored, as she will always make it clear that she does not associate with failures. These kinds of mothers push their children too hard to not think of anything else except the next best car, phone, etc.

How To Get Over A Narcissist

When you're dating a narcissist, everything revolves around them. It's both perplexing and stressful. Finally, you muster the courage to depart one day. While this is an exciting time for you since you are heading on the right path, there is a difficult transition following a split with a narcissist. It's not simple to get over a narcissist just because they treat you like garbage. In fact, this is one of the most challenging types of breakups to overcome. You have ups and downs on a regular basis—as it's if your relationship is on a roller coaster. So here's how to end your relationship with a narcissist for good.

1. Stop obsessing.

Because it's practically difficult to establish a relationship with a narcissist, you spent a lot of time dissecting their behavior and character in order to make sense of the curveballs they kept tossing at you. Unfortunately, this compulsive pattern of analysis will continue after you leave an abusive relationship until you push it to stop.

Remind yourself that you are no longer concerned about your ex and gently urge your mind to focus on something else whenever ideas about what's wrong with them come—rep to this process as needed. According to most experts, changing a habit takes three months.

2. Avoid trying to rationalize.

To maintain the peace and justify sticking with your narcissist through all those dysfunctional challenges, you had to make excuses for their conduct, minimize their abuse, reinterpret their falsehoods, and tiptoe around their self-delusions. You'll start reasoning again when you miss them now—and you will— thinking, "Oh, they're not that horrible."

Don't get taken in by it. Instead, remind yourself why you left to prevent being influenced by your narcissistic ex or, worse, falling back in love with them. Maintaining zero touches is the best method to achieve this. Block them on social media and don't contact or text them. There's a reason why most experts recommend following the no-contact rule. We'll go over that in more detail after this list.

3. **Find ways to cope with your anxiety.**

Your nervous system is probably still functioning along those lines because your narcissist had you on edge for months or years. Leaving might also trigger new stressors or worries, exacerbating your anxiety. Furthermore, sex has ceased, so you no longer have the dopamine and oxytocin that were keeping your head above water.

Yoga, dancing, swimming, and other forms of exercise are all good options.

Every day, whenever you need it, do something.

4. **Keep busy.**

A relationship with a narcissist is all about power. You don't have it; they do. You scurry around, attempting to normalize everything, but you never achieve because they want you to scurry so they can jerk your chain anytime they want. This sounds awful, and it was, but it did help pass the time. There's a vast, empty gap in your days now that no one is doing it. Life isn't quite as interesting as it once was.

To cope, constantly exploring new hobbies and activities, and make an effort to spend as much time as possible with your pals. If you must stay at home, use meditation to relax your thoughts. Know that you don't have to search outside for happiness; you can find it within yourself.

5.   Don't blame yourself.

You're probably remorseful for covering your eyes for so long now that you can see your ex for the narcissist they were and recognize how detrimental the actions you engaged in for so long were. You might wonder how you came to be so "naive," "stupid," or "gullible." You may feel particularly bad if you're around family or friends who were tuned in long before you were.

Allow yourself some time to relax. You're only human, and narcissists are seduction masters. You may dig into your codependency and self-esteem issues when you're in a better place, but for now, just forgive yourself. It's critical to keep in mind that your ignorance is a good thing. It implies that you have an open and trusting heart, something your narcissist lacks.

6. Focus on self-love.

Because one of the narcissist's methods is to knock people down in order to elevate themselves, you're unlikely to have received any praise, support, or gratitude once the seduction period ended. You may have also been subjected to verbal abuse. Because narcissists want you to be insecure, feeling confident in yourself is a foreign concept to you right now. As a result of being gaslighted for so long, you may have lost faith in your own judgment.

What's the best place to start recovering from all of this? Therapists, self-help programs, and support groups may all help you focus on self-love, which is what you need to do to rebuild your self-esteem after a breakup. Find a regular meetup with a group of individuals who are interested in the same sort of personal development as you are.

7. Prioritize your pleasure.

Many problematic relationships rely on sex because connection and emotional fulfillment aren't accessible, according to research. Narcissists, in particular, like using sex as a powerful weapon because they want addicts who need to be wanted. So they keep your desire alive by distributing sexual "affection" in accordance with their own power-driven goal. So, even if your relationship was steamy, you'll still want them sexually. It's simply a reality.

What are your options for coping? Select a high-quality vibrator. Your emotional vampire of an ex isn't any more devoid of human love, empathy, or compassion than that piece of plastic.

8. Acknowledge your jealousy.

Most narcissists replace their ex-girlfriends or boyfriends within weeks, if not days, following their breakup, typically from a stable they've kept stocked during your relationship. Remember that they must always have a source of energy to feed on. They make certain that their supply is safe at all times. You can feel that you're just an arrangement that stopped being handy when you stopped accepting abuse because they struggle with healthy attachment and true feelings of connection. Regardless of who they catch next, it will just be a better business transaction.

When you're feeling envious, remember that those poor individuals are getting set up the same way you were, and they're going to suffer in the end. Convert your enmity toward them into compassion.

9.   Stop looking back.

You might be asking why you wasted so much time with your narcissist if you stayed with them for an extended period of time. And if you've piled up a lot of debt for them or are the parent of their children, you've got a lot more on your plate than just squandered time.

The most important thing is that you survived. I'm trying not to look back and instead focus on what I'm developing for the future. It's impossible to live a human life without regrets, as any wise elder would tell you.

10. Let yourself grieve.

All of the measures above will not alleviate your aching heart, but they will modify your actions and set in action new dynamics to assist you to prevent relapsing. Grief is a lengthy and delicate process that comes and goes, sometimes for years, in the mending of the human heart.

Spend some time honoring your loss by looking underneath your anger for the sadness. Recognize the process of inviting yourself back home as you soothe yourself. Feel glad for the feelings you've had to hold in for years, even if they've been tough. They can finally come out now that you're with someone who loves and accepts you for who you are—yourself!

Steps to Toward Codependency Recovery

While codependency is a very challenging behavioral pathology, the good W news is that it is definitely something that one can heal and transcend.

To do this requires a solid commitment to change one's patterns of thinking and action and hard work, and a dependable support system. In order to make lasting changes, you must realize that the process of healing is ongoing—you will likely never reach a place where you are perfect and have no more need for improvement.

However, with a sincere commitment and consistent efforts, you will soon see drastic improvements that will immediately lead to a healthier and happier life.

While the road to recovery is in no way easy, it offers profound rewards and has the power to free you from much unnecessary suffering, fear, and unhappiness that you had taken to be an ordinary part of life. The truth is that codependent ways of living are not necessary and not inevitable. As you change your innermost patterns and false beliefs, you may find a new life opening up for you and your close relationships.

Codependency Addiction Recovery is stopping the cycle of codependency. It may seem daunting, but it is very possible. There are countless steps you can take if you decide to take the initiative.

Here are many of the most effective measures you can take to recover from codependence:

Reality Check

The first thing you absolutely have to take is to look at your reality and your situation with a realistic lens. Denial is one of the most horrible enemies of healing and recovery, so sit yourself down and survey your case and your relationship without sugarcoating anything. Knowing all aspects of a problem is the first step towards solving it, so do so with care. Though it may be difficult, know that you are about to begin a journey of healing and recovery.

While you analyze your situation, it's also vital that you avoid blaming yourself for what's happened in the past. Go as much as possible to think in a rational way and avoid focusing on things like regret or things you should have done differently.

Acceptance

Aside from giving yourself a reality check, you also need to accept the things you have realized about the situation. As with the previous point, denial can only serve to bring you harm. Therefore, the next step you need to take is to accept what has happened to you and decide how to move on for the better.

Recognize Your Role

Though it may be easy to blame your partner for everything that went wrong in your relationship, this is often not the case. It's also vital that you recognize what you could have done differently and what weaknesses prevented you from breaking free of codependency. Doing so doesn't mean that you can now start self-blame. Recognizing your role simply means that you identify what aspects of yourself you can improve upon to strengthen things that can help you avoid falling back into bad habits and relationships.

Internal Vs. External

One important factor that you need to realize is that recovery from codependence is mostly an internal process. Before taking any additional steps, you need to realize that you need to focus internally rather than looking to external sources or other people to "fix" you.

Recovering from codependency means recovering yourself; your values, your needs, your feelings, your wants, and your own identity. These can only come from within.

See the Positive

A recent study has shown that showing gratitude can actually make a person happier and more content. Though your past may be negative or hurtful, it's important that you try and identify the aspects of your life you can be grateful for. This will help you remain positive and will help give you hope that not everything in your life is damaged. There is constantly something to hope for, and finding these things in your life can help you significantly on your road to recovery.

Abstain

Much like any addiction, you need to be able to abstain from what is keeping you addicted. The same concept can be applied to codependency. It's important that one of the steps you take is to try and maintain some distance from your partner or the person that is weighing you down.

Safety and Precaution

In line with the previous point, remember to take great precautions in making your safety the main priority. Remember that codependent relationships can easily be abusive. If you are a victim of physical, emotional, or domestic abuse, it's vital that you first determine your "escape route" or where you can go in case of emergency.

If you feel you are at risk or in harm's way, you need to inform those close to you about what you plan to do. If and when you confront your partner, you need to make sure that you have people you can go to in order to keep safe. This is especially important if you have children with you.

Confront Your Partner

Once you set up a safe environment, make sure that you let your partner know what you're going through. It's important that you are able to confront the problem you are facing, and more often than not, your partner is a big part of that. Expressing yourself to a person who has kept you suppressed is not only vindicating but is also greatly freeing. It is an important step in recovery and can help you fully move from focusing on others to concentrate on taking care of yourself.

Again, however, take this step with a grain of salt. If you feel that you will be putting yourself in serious danger by confronting your partner, it's crucial that you have people with you to remove you from the situation in case things get hostile. Make sure that the confrontation happens in a neutral place where exits are easily accessible.

Visualize

One of the most necessary steps in solving a problem is also knowing your goals and what you want. Therefore, it's vital to visualize yourself in a better place in your relationships and general well-being. This will also help you recover in terms of getting back to who you are and getting to know yourself again.

Challenge Negativity

A common problem that codependent people encounter is having negative thoughts about themselves. This contributes to generally impaired self-worth and keeps a person trapped in abusive situations. Therefore, challenging these negative thoughts is a vital component to recovering from codependency.

A perfect way to do this is to question and analyze whether these thoughts are grounded in reality. For example, if you begin to think that you are incompetent, ask yourself what evidence is there if your inadequacy.

Did you really do anything to warrant these thoughts? Asking rational questions will help you realize that these negative thoughts are actually unfounded and that there isn't room to entertain these kinds of thoughts in daily living.

Stop the Labels

Codependent individuals often label themselves or listening to labels that other people give them. In order to battle codependency, you need to fight the urge to give yourself labels based on your mistakes or based on how others perceive you. When you find labels forming in your thoughts, consciously shift your thoughts to something more positive. Rather than calling yourself "incompetent," change this to something more constructive, like recognizing yourself as a "work in progress."

Self-Monitor

A necessary step in recovery is to closely monitor your own thoughts and your own self-perception. When you find yourself making mistakes or feeling down, respond with compassion rather than self-blame. Think about other times you have been challenged and the times you were able to overcome the various difficulties you've encountered. Remind yourself that you are tough and that you deserve to be free of abuse and codependency.

Self-monitoring is very useful in that you are able to prevent negative thoughts from escalating into more severe forms of depression or low selfesteem. Keeping a journal of your thoughts can also give you a solid record, something that you can look over to see how you've improved and to know what you need to work on even more.

Manage Your Recovery Process

Recovery can be daunting, and backsliding isn't uncommon. Therefore, it's important that you take things step-by-step. Compartmentalize and break up the recovery process into manageable tasks so as not to get overwhelmed. Set particular functions that you need to complete in a set amount of time. Try to limit yourself to accomplishing that task within the given time, at a reasonable pace. This will help prevent frustration and will allow you time to recover in a manageable way.

Seek Professional Help

Though many victims of codependency find it challenging to approach professionals for help, know that coming to a counselor or psychologist is nothing to be ashamed of. These professionals can greatly help you navigate the murky waters of recovery and help you sort out what has happened to you in the past. Having an objective party to talk to can also give you a special point of view, one that helps you see angles of the situation that may have been formerly unknown to you.

Celebrate Small Victories

A large part of recovering from codependency is regaining control over your life, and letting the sunshine in, so to speak. A great method to do this is to celebrate the small successes and small victories that you've experienced.

For example, rewarding yourself after finishing a difficult task at work may seem like a small thing, but it serves as a building block to your new foundation of self-esteem and positive self-regard. These all add up and all contribute to building a better you.

Engage In New Things

Engaging in new activities and pursuing new things will help you get back to your roots and assist you in your self-improvement journey. Focus on yourself by finding out what you're good at, discovering what you enjoy, and indulge in activities that contribute to your own development. This will not only help you become better but will also help you recover from the pain of your past. A positive effect of trying out new things and mastering new skills is that these give you something that you can consider your own and can give you accomplishments that you can be proud of. Furthermore, these will help you gain a sense of independence that is much needed to combat codependency.

Pamper Yourself

Part of recovery is to indulge in your own needs and wants. Being in a codependent relationship can really exhaust you and your resources. Therefore, recovery is a time dedicated to taking care of yourself. One way to heal is to indulge and pamper yourself by doing things you love the most and reconnecting with what you want outside of your relationships. Remember that you don't need other people to feel good about yourself, and one way to do so is to start caring for yourself rather than putting everyone else's satisfaction ahead of yours.

Contribute to Social Good

One great way of bolstering positivity and feeling better about life, in general, is contributing to projects of social good. Therefore, try to engage in projects and events that help others, such as a local feed the homeless program, raising donations for charities, etc.

Reconnect

A common symptom of codependence is isolating oneself from loved ones and support networks. If you've distanced yourself from those you love and those who love you, then know that a vital step to recovery is re-establishing these ties with the people who matter most. Those who genuinely care for you will push you to be better and will encourage you to rebuild yourself no matter how challenging.

Conclusion

Are you able to recognize and comprehend you are surrounded by bad energy and continue to make decisions based on it if you are aware of the "Law of Attraction"? What good can come from the narcissist emotional abuser's or your continued involvement in anything that is negative? Your assumption that continuing in this "imaginary" relationship will lead to your death is entirely incorrect. There isn't a single good concept or image in mind.

One of the reasons you've stayed in this bad circumstance is that you're well aware of how much emotional anguish you're in today. Leaving what you have with the narcissist emotional abuser would entail intentionally creating suffering, and you're already hurting so much you're not sure how much more you can take. But you know that if you give it a few more hours or days, it won't be a week, the love of your life will offer you more of what you don't think you can manage. So you're aware of it.

You're caught in the center of your hope, unable to move. So let's re-evaluate your hope's emphasis. You hope that you will be able to maintain what you have and that things will change in the future, allowing you to be free of emotional agony.

You're in a lot of emotional agonies right now, and you know that being with the narcissist emotional abuser will be the last of you. You've reached the point when you must take a chance. Why don't you take the 'risk of survival?' You'll be OK.